How to be Hungry

Stu Hatton was born in Boston, England in 1977, and since 1986 has lived in Melbourne, Australia. He holds a BA from the University of Melbourne and an MA from Deakin University, where he teaches writing and editing. Since 2005 he has also worked in research into drug use, young people's use of health services, and depression.

www.stuhatton.net

How to be Hungry

Stu Hatton

First published in 2010 by (outer)

Front cover image: 'Green Bomb' by Psychonaught.
Back cover image courtesy of the DEA.

National Library of Australia
Cataloguing-in-Publication data

Hatton, Stu 1977-.
How to be Hungry.

1st ed.
ISBN 978-1-4466-3133-1 (pbk.).

I. Title.

A821.4

www.stuhatton.net

www.lulu.com

For Monica

Acknowledgements

I would like to thank my wife Monica, my parents and all of my family and friends for your love and support.

Thanks to my teachers, mentors and fellow writers for encouragement, advice and criticism along the way. And to the editors of the books, journals, zines and e-zines where some of these poems first appeared, usually in earlier incarnations.

Special thanks to Tom Clark and Alexia Maddox for looking over the manuscript and offering helpful suggestions.

I would also like to thank the Australian Society of Authors for offering the mentorship I undertook with Dorothy Porter throughout 2007. As I've acknowledged elsewhere, Dorothy's advice was crucial for the development of this book, and continues to resonate. So last of all, though she is no longer with us, I would like to thank Dorothy, for everything.

contents

This is the noble truth of the origin of suffering: it is this craving ... accompanied by delight and lust, seeking delight here and there, that is, craving for sensual pleasures, craving for existence, craving for extermination.

- The Buddha

… a most cruel insanity has warped your mind;
While drugs may well have caused it, they can bring no cure.

- as spoken by Teiresias in Euripides' *The Bacchae*

We have drunk the soma; we have become immortals, we have gone to the light; we have found the gods.

- *The Rig Veda*

drowse

1.
dirt & dust cling
to abandoned adhesive
(a sticker once spoke here)

2.
the wall's layers of skin:
obsolete gig posters
discoloured, torn

3.
schoolkids escape to the city,
get into all kinds of circuitry

4.
the sushi bar radio's
misheard lyrics:
'let's unrest
our babyloooooooove'
(???)

5.
everyone coughing up
these tiny pips of happiness
that crunch underfoot

6.
while you, the stay-at-home,
sleep through the heat …
bubbles of spittle
pop on your teeth

drive-thru

The radio sniffling some song out, and
its candy glare seduces us, drawing
conversation to the fringes, as cigarette
ash rains from the wound-down windows,
the car idling beside the backlit menu,

touched-up burgers, magnified fries.
Queuing up in the drive-thru we're itchy,
as if we're watching lottery balls land while
chewing our tickets; but our order is easy:
to wind up muted, forgotten, satisfied.

We bin the cups & wraps, waste more cigarettes,
then drive ... through a streak of green lights
that flick to late amber, past sullen drivers
tapping fingers on steering wheels,
windscreens snatching warped ghosts.

And the zebra crossings stripe under us,
as the radio station goes off the air, and
we are handed over to the silence, as a
speed camera gets another dumb picture,
its diamond flash dribbles off the car.

stem

if rain falls it is imperceptible.

*

longing to be left alone in our many rooms.

*

stem overgrown with thought. seated in lotus position.

*

we map disappearances. small birds wrapped daily. cannot drink the river.

*

rowing three hours each way between us. to arrive at degrees of fidelity. granting the eye permission to lick.

*

think we're coping better with crop failures. though there are times we want to murder the fruit. unpeel what is peeled. how we never know how to hold what's dying.

*

our housedust. a lint magnet. stem the breath with fluff. dustmites fed on skinflakes.

*

if the rain would pile upon itself. if the harvest. bring breath to what is spoken.

*

lotus position. the spine a stem.

*

to err. planting the heart. longing to be left alone. listening for dry echo.

*

to say ‘tremble then. break with the room. strew dust. be spilt.’

*

to say ‘stay faithful. wear blue on blue days.’

the breaking

the shatter & melt:

glass filled with ice
slipped from my hand.

i mean, i was
just flaking in a booth, dimlit bar,
3 friends,
drugs between us making mistakes

&
didn't want to know
your whereabouts
how you were captured
what painkillers stomached
what beds caught you
when you fell.

i fell till 10am,
blurred in cabs, throwing money;
crashed some dirty-hive recovery

glued to girl,
dosed up & vodkas,
flapping mothlikc at the lights,
kamikaze.

played
dumb, played
dead

& in her eyes,
death that pretty young thing,
saw a way in.

cashed

was cashed up dangling fifties hundreds over the bar lights shallow red amber faces firing chronic my good friend Greg conjuring joints sparking up /

smoked up zoned loosed selecting fancy cocktails from fancy menu talking up tweaking with tongue letting it flick & lash bringing the punchline in to land timing it tight being such sophists drawing attention dwarfing our usual shrunken selves spying those libertine women so *dressed* thinking they're spies like us /

my good friend Greg on the phone hooked up to the apparatus trying to hook us trying for 350 for cut 400 for pure pureish wallet prepped in position are we good we're good to go yeah Johnny will be here in 20 what a guy

unplugged

day two of rehab

the raw bed
no exits
air soured by puke

steel-cold/sleepless,
fingers heavy with days

deserted eyes
lucid-dream:
running city steam-alleys
to cut a repair deal

ever try a sprint lying down?
(it's exhausting)

& the stories i stowed in the city
have scattered, escaped into films
(my brainchild their goldmine)

*

outside of visiting hrs
a squad of ghosts
makes another sweep

Vipassanā

Meditation
shouldn't be misunderstood
as another search for an exit

It is a way back
to where you are

First letting the eyes stop,
calming the antennae

Then all punctuation dropped,
an unhurried torch
shone throughout the body

The mind does not need to shop

Silent as smoke
except for the radio
from the apartment below,
bleeps counting in the newshour;
swooshes of traffic, birdsong solos,
hum of the nearby city

Of course the body hands out flyers
for a protest march
and sometimes a slow bee visits,
buzzing at every itch,
every knot of fear,
every burn of venom in the blood

The ongoing task of sitting
may be learning such restlessness
by heart
(the heart has many commas)
while mind writes smaller and smaller

Though my first teacher taught
that mind and heart are the same bell,
fused in a single word:
chitta

draft wording for revolution : from balcony at Blue Train Café

riverside : the CBD a 3D graph : bright-coloured banners of Southbank fatten in wind : no one swims the Yarra : 'who in their right mind would even *paint* a river that colour?'

Blue Train kitchen clatters like tournament knights : reject the see-saw table we're shown to : pull more napkins than needed : #4 pizza

we fidget, blag : 'how many secret lives are played?' : graduates of the self-help section : get an edge : no handholds : bust a critique : 'can't kick can't run can't tackle' : how we got mired in fandom

conversation slips political : bluff through buzzword city : '*are you for real*?' : tad earnest : 'could you ever love a patriot?' : wave stats like flags while we jiggle teabags

mark this urgent : sale must end! : stocktake : 'could you feed our world while we're away?' : planet's lungs morph into soya beans : amazon dot gone : hybrid seeds won't reproduce

we brainstorm : waves form waveforms : floodfill the notepad : a few words of our own : can beat them on paper : *we can be heroes*

cut to Planet America : juicer linebackers built like tanks : big fish with big guns : and we, blind photographers

kidding ourselves : 'sorry speak up I can't quite …' : 'another drink?' : gales of laughter : 'sorry kids, we're gonna need this table …'

fallback : resolve split in the sore spot : so rooted, futures dim pedestrian : how we slide : soak all night in unmarked bars

power ballad

who is ever still,
   here in the live feed?

(could go every way)

peering at decisions,
   drinks list

she pierces the yolk-bubble,
   dribbles yellow

everyone loves to be ignored,
   nonchalant or chalant
      swooping on ignorance

days when you don't want your name
   associated

the future's correct,
   be so sure

fiction wins

'augmented reality'
   a letdown
      (teleprompter ≠ teleporter)

night opens to speed,
   farms out fragments
      raided by addicts

placebo's 'pure morning'
   a tweaker anthem,
      meth's power ballad

crystal methamphetamine,
   a naked eraser

post-rock

milk a baby black box recorder weaving through a vista mural in much clusters exposé of the fast wind chimes anecdotal with hard data spectral of course whitewater it's a soundtrack to the abandoning the good stuff kids go a film does coke thankfully bottles fabric of the desert beginning or end melancholia the source of uncertainty friends of small eternities so well-suited to employ them scissors inverted in such a wide-eared though bookish it's surprising it's taken so long onstage as a longtime fan for this trick of exposure emblematically more attention beautiful greyscale as one might expect tracks of quilted feedback nonetheless manage to breathe like premature a blob of goopy a few insane years people were ant traffic through forced windows out front lush vocal harmonies groove officer and texture middling big-sky arranged into the shape of the obligatory close-ups

the masculine

poor pathetic male. spend the whole day jerking off. would opt out if you could. what awaits discovery here? no black gold. what's a man without it? downing a slab of mid-strength. what're a few uncried tears? while diving in ink. don't bother looking down there. it's nothing, always nothing. who's alpha? is this what you have left to offer? even your pen refuses to write. the bastard. what you will resort to. you shop around. in hell's name. for endgames. speed chess is the game for you? they queue for your time. 'not for sale' sticker attracts attention. you'd love to crack. somewhere bright & crowded. with family units. michael douglas in *falling down*. a good career move. tear their smiles off. c'mon you're far too meek. take it out on an ornament. assault by proxy. hurl down a galaxy of glass.

WA Notebook

I – coastal

‘too hot to get busy anyway’

unused sky bestowing confidence

we’ll take the coastal road

Aussie flags hoisted on roofs, in sandy gardens

‘fuck off we’re full’ sticker
                    on a ute’s rear panel

letting the sunset beach do the tender talking

the brewery will do the rest

the sea:
          yet more fields to be farmed

parasails sweep, flip
                        as tankers ride the horizon

– on the coastal road to Fremantle, Western Australia

II – *development*

impermeable, unstirred, unmoved

these lives that go on regardless

city of satellites

another new suburb on the city fringe

mounds of sand, industrial supplies stand waiting

shopping village has the works for home and garden

'we'll need at least 15 bags of ice'

the hells these cuts of meat came through (you'd weep & refuse to eat)

driving past these oversize words that say nothing, nothing to stop us

'what lifting the ban on uranium mining would do for this state'

news item portraying protesters as terrorists / clowns / mutants

this station plays the golden oldies

– Ellenbrook, Western Australia

III – *waterfront*

subdued table

lunch overheated / flavourless

running the risk of being asked to leave –
    shouldn't be eating this food here
    though no sign forbids it

the *bona fide* clientele stab their disapproval
    without so much as eye contact

this place swallowed by sun & ice cream kids
    boats knocking against the quay
    playground throbbing with fluro noise

a drink could make things worse

in the car park cars melting /
    wavelets shimmer on windshields

– Hilarys Boat Harbour, Western Australia

IV – *the days write themselves*

A roadsign warns: golf buggies crossing.
Listen: is that a shot off the fairway
or a big bloke preparing to spit?
Perhaps both. Grey roos
bound out of sandtraps.
No one is making this up. Really
the days write themselves.
There'll be folks over at 5
for champagne & nibbles.
Then the Monday after the 60th bash
we'll fit in 9 holes.
Stocked up so much alcohol
the house begins to sink. And
the parrots don't want us here either.
Not as if they need our help
to be classy. Who owns this plot
of blue & cirrus sky? Flies
routinely circle the heat
of the road. 4x4s rocket past
as we retreat into slim roadside shade.
Grasshoppers broadcast dry static.

– *The Vines, Western Australia*

V – *these bastions of quiet achievement*

What can be said here?
Passing a school
& two churches,
a dozen placards
tout success.
Truly,
'this plot of land was sold
by Candice Weymouth.' She
looks happy, but
what choice does she have?
Systemic smile.

space at a premium fill it
while you can please call

All we're asking for is
sedated children,
by which we mean our own
or those seated nearby
(having paid top dollar
for these seats). 'Sorry this is
such a one-sided
conversation;
I'm genuinely interested
in what you have thought.
What you think
when you're not thinking,
how you swim as you drown.'

– Scarborough, Western Australia

VI – *departing*

post-dawn
red sun   pinks the hills
out the passenger window   winery country
signposted gourmet tours

columns of vapour   rising   over pools
& the Swan too   as we bridge over it

this early   only airport traffic
rows of dormant yellow earthmovers
bobcats for hire

these lives we will never lead
laid out dead before us

fashionably

time I reach the party
all the drugs
have already been played
(a recurring theme)

my selfish friends!
I just wanted a little toy-toy for *me*!!!

to let the drugs
do the talking

get the monkey off,
write myself *on*

okay, *I'll* drop the code
if *you'll* quit coding with *me*

all you can offer
is flattery
& these wedges of lime

sure, there's booze & pot
(downers covered)
like you said

but watch me
clear the dancefloor

it's like I arrive &
everyone's leaving,
whispering 'life's too short
for this dreck'

leaves me no choice but
to steal your lines,
drink you dry,
crashland on your couch:

when you kick me awake
I'll be itching,
pestering you

to make that call
(fingers crossed),
drive across town for pills

repackaging 'evil'

on the track to the city
a snake says 'trust me',
and what could be
simpler? it's just an
advertisement, though
clearly everyone
is implicated

/ way the ads burst
volumed at our outer
skin nudge the inner
what big hoofs more
than a little tampering
with our brittle

/ forever
overtowered by cranes
fishing for significance
will spill our dossiers
as if 'connect' means my
brand is your brand but
i can't get no, no no no

retreat

each morning
the gong waking us
into 4:30am darkness

*

for the first three days
watching the breath

*

feel breath entering
& leaving the nostrils,
channels of breath
lightly brushing
the upper lip

*

stripped of speech
& gesture
how we still keep
a polite distance,
how I am careful
not to slurp at my tea
in the dining hall

*

writing is not permitted;
‘there is no need
to take notes’

*

no reading material
except signs & notices;
a makeshift sign
on the border of the property reads
‘do not go beyond this point’

*

every day after breakfast
walking alone through the field;
around its perimeter
the long grass has been trampled
into a narrow path;
my toes & sandals
sprayed with dew;
cicadas leaping
away from each step

*

perhaps a sleepmurmur
is all that has exited
my mouth for days –
other than a cough
or froth of toothpaste

*

three times a day
a 'sitting of determination':
to remain still
for an hour,
observing the pain
in shoulders & spine
as it arises

*

hearing only
the anticipated chant
that will signal
hour's end

*

nearing the hour
the coughing starts up
amongst the men
meditating around me

*

remembered songs drop by,
wash uninvited through
the meditating mind

*

what is that sound?
the knocking
of two percussive blocks
or a frog
restless in the dawn?

*

4:30am
New Year's Day:
close to 40 degrees celsius;
moths, mosquitoes, others
drunken in the heat,
revel around the nightlight
outside the dorm.

*

some afternoons
must be 45 degrees
in the meditation hall;
leaving a sweat-lake
on the mat

*

break my vow of silence
to inform the manager
that the first toilet on the left
has a blockage

*

men & women segregated,
separate facilities,
though we all meditate

in the same hall –
men to the left,
women to the right

*

everyone asked to dress ‘modestly’
to minimise distractions

*

meditating in the hall
at dusk,
intermittent mooing
of a distant cow

*

sleepless:
a spider on the window
of the dorm ...
this side of the glass

*

without communication
it’s difficult
to reach any agreement:
whether the dorm door
should be open or closed
during sleeping hours

*

on white porcelain sinks
in the washroom,
mosquitoes & beetles:
a growing collection of corpses

*

anicca:
all things arise,
pass away

*

the instruction
repeated:
'Start again.
Start again ...'

driving hours

reading dust
signatures

communication
of the road

we blur
trees

’92 mixtape,
landscape
mix

until we tire
of music

too-loud talkback vowels
when the tape
ejects

engine drone
hazes stale exchange

*

we stop
to wake

truckstop
litter
overflow

reminded by
the occasional
bird

*

driving out
of night

everything
vibrates,
the stars

even through
the petrol stop

no stills

*

motel mattress
tremors

remember
how to sleep?

air-con
insomnia

highway
still straining
south

flashing down
to the border

forkhead
(After David Lynch's *Lost Highway*)

There there. You're tired. Stressed. Have collected no victories. All your curfews. Even the sax hasn't let you out. Of the house. But I'm there right now. Call me.

*

This must be super-rare, but the first time I saw *Lost Highway* I was stoned. Foreseeing a headfilm, I'd shared a preparatory J outside the theatre. Finding my seat, I found myself quietly toasted.

*

Forks in the road, in the head. Highways by night; snaking lights. Lost in forks.

*

An ancient book on the art of feigning death. Unquenchable book.

*

From early in the piece I had Fred Madison figured as a fellow forkhead. A real channelsurfer. My suspicions were confirmed (bigtime) when he forked into parallel identities, Fred Madison becoming Pete Dayton becoming Fred Madison becoming, etc.

*

More questions than answers: he wears black or black wears him? Who's tailgating who? How would he hide his body around himself, resurface out of the corners of her? Whaddayou mean, 'What?!'

*

The phone's ringing. (Again). Odd,

*

Hello …?

*

LH formed a double bill with *Dead Man*. Lynch's film came first, with its rapid eye movement. The good confusion. By the time it was over I had little energy for Jim Jarmusch's film … in my sleepwatching was left to ponder whether *LH* could equally have been titled *Dead Man*.

*

Entertainment as sleep? Psychotropic celluloid. Inks run in drawers. The woman who isn't a doppelganger. (Where is she?)

*

Plant cameras in the dark, rich soil. Houseplants that require no natural light. (Pupils dilate). Footage blooms in the night.

*

We've met before, haven't we? This being one of those lines that must be quoted 'in character'.

*

Impossible to say the story's over. Just as it's impossible to say, 'The story's over there.' Still, despite everyone's best intentions, the story may be put to rest with a cliché. A time-marker. The post-film cigarette, with its rush of switching back to some kind of

*

Gate left open. Video cassette on the steps.

café date

coffee kicks

your date
talks your arm off

you yet another
imitation audience

such expertise in
appearing unconfused

even when your attention swings
to the drizzle of adjectives
out on the street

& how do you like
these café clientele

glazed cakes &
tarts under glass

sincere, unimpressed looks
that say, ‘I hope
you are not the future’

don’t they realise
the number of errors
can only inflate?

you drop a twenty
on the table,
slip out alone

telltale

bloodshots (red cables cross my eyes) –
telltale,
obvious i've used

lip-cracks / foodless sta-
sis / cold-core bones

afternoon: slight OD,
fell asleep online

evening:
you arrive home /
my straight act:
no trace,
paraphernalia locked away /
affectionate lies

rain

1.
no one takes his leaflets –
why? because it's raining?

2.
this weather
is a lot of information

3.
tense as glass this morning
as he sits to meditate

4.
subtle sensations of *vipassanā*:
isolated showers

5.
his hand will not destroy
even the smallest creatures

6.
someone jokes
that his hand lacks teeth

7.
his apartment
becomes a moth colony

8.
this rain
is unintentional

9.
naked he stands,
a book in each hand

10.
smiling, shaping to accept,
he enters the rain

Portrait of Ledong Qui

Fuelling the party
is a man from Manchuria
with lampshade hat –
in his worker's bag
a bottle of 60% *baijiu*
with Chinese characters
partying on the label;
one shareable shot glass;
a fishbowl jar of aniseed beans
soaked grey like fishbowl pebbles;
and a bag of sunflower seeds
which he says are to be eaten
'like a bird' eats, and staying true
to his word, leaves seedhusks
strewn to mark his perching –
41 amongst late-twentysomethings,
dignified in specs,
'wise old man of the East'
(he laughs at this!) –
he in turn fuelled by
poetry, philosophy, psych-jazz,
the detuned,
the random.

He crashes at ours, contributes $2
to the cab, leaves a note marked 9:15am
saying thankyou, and that
the day has greatness to be had.

meeting

You start to get a feel for what might be expected
at this level. Those around the table who
intimidate you do so only out of habit. Whether
or not to move on to the next item appears to be
the key point for debate. Amidst coughing, nods
and cultured laughter you stoop to distrusting your
acumen; your assertions falter, drowned by those
in smoother humour. You are once again amazed
at how much you don't know, at your allergic
response to operational matters. You know
you wouldn't want to be left one-on-one
with any of those seated here; conversation
is for others. Continually looking to the clock
for lenience, you plan to slip away during lunch
& not return to the room for the resumption. Your
hand trembles as you reach for a biscuit.

digitalia

every day here
at the image farm

dum-dee-dum ...
crop & resize

shrinking into, becoming
synonymous with my work

am this low-cost 'virtusurgery'

am 'his' & 'her' sightlines

*

every day here
looking for some other face

out in the data rain,
packet traffic

not another me for chrissakes

some unique visitor
with cowled, smoky needs

to feign interest,
sabotage my inbox?

*

photograph is a spell,
curse

seductively true

*

deskrider
pumping the brakes

(praying for
glue to meld the storm together)

I am a fat,
balding forgery

swipe-card
at hip

free of the fear of freedom

one who flows

is a flower

scratches

’Burb.
The monadic life.
Bird’s call a greeting / warning / reminder.

*

Caged food.
E. coli.
Filed sewage.

*

Live a little less filtered?
Who has time for these experiments?

*

Crossword clue: ‘experimental’; solution: ‘tentative’.

*

Automatic door won’t acknowledge.
As if you don’t have a million things to steer.

*

Mouthing around for endearment, closure.

*

No recipient.

*

Scratch eczema till bleeding.
As if narrative were inevitable.

*

Monkish nest.
Fallen into the hands of Buddhists.

‘Bit too life-affirming for me.’

*

No audience for preachers here.

*

Step foot in these political premises.
Dogshit.

*

Public imagery.

*

Lowlife.
Shy collectors.
Sniped upskirt.

*

Airbrushed avatar.

*

Default emotion?

*

Make no attempt.
Nothing to talk to.

*

Learning how to be uncomfortable.
Suffocating new scenery.
Who doesn’t attract weirdos?

*

Easy exit.
Must go, before we become friends.

*

Chickened.

*

Do not thank the owner when leaving.

*

What benefit of hindsight?

*

Milk-fed.
32, afraid.
Tendril of half-bitten mouthflesh at the jawline.

*

A sign: ‘No pukers’.

*

Eyes avert from the flashforward.

*

Imposed structure.
Trained garden.
Need poems.

*

Of uncertain authorship.
omnium gatherum.

*

Pump omens into?

*

You may yet prove interesting.
Or ... not.

*

'We are happy to inform you.'

*

Dear Repeater.
You are a collection.
Don't worry.

*

Pill wears off.
Nothing learned once that doesn't need learning again.

*

To 'overcome' desire.
To 'overcome' writing.
Posing an endpoint poses a problem.

mnml

scramble 3am sunday the club
at our most intelligent
hyperchoiced feel enhancer
micro-level the sequenced
lighting sweeping floor in
petalshapes kid behind the
decks from paris no don't
bow he's coolly laying glitch
on glitch you love this
thudder hihats snipping you are
this unique visitor back soon
re-embodied score one for ads
without products planetary
maps rolled out for the
breakdown wait the warm
silence teaser spinback till 18-
wheeler leaden kickdrum cuts
the surface re-entry timed to

Three Brett Whiteleys

I - *Art, Life and The Other Thing*

They don't know you. Any of you.
Your death, perhaps, but how many
know your brush? Hardly blame them.
(Re-check the time. Art is late.)
                                        Though
your balcony still stands, like a debt:
sunlit, public. I would drink coffee there, & write,
& later let something summer tunnel me: liquid
lime or lemon, glass jug reefed with ice.
Maybe light a smoke, though I quit
years ago.
          Sydney Harbour lies back
getting sucked off by a tall,
professional sun. Glitter harbour,
waves winking like flecks of mica in asphalt;
& consider other flaky metaphors where the
'natural' vies with the manufactured (swarmed
metaphors clip wings, tailspin). Everything
poised at a silent point in conversation. That word:
poise ... propeller it in your fingers like a biro.
The other thing would be sweet. It's
days ablaze like these that the whole ritual of
dessert makes sense, & you think, 'Who needs it?',
drown it in double cream. Art & life are fine:
you're happy to camp out in the rubble,
only senile gods for company,
and sure, the sky makes a fine tent,
but ... you know. You know it.
                                  Nails lined up,
tapped with the care of a close shave,
driven! in! flush!
               Clawed out warped   is art.

II - *Self Portrait After Three Bottles of Wine*

Christ!
        Gulf between nothing doing & doing
nothing (about 3 bottles wide).
                                        No quicker learner(!),
this pissed hound of instinct. One of those nights
spent swallowing the urge to score.
You may never be Brett Whiteley,
but he's with you on the toilet wall,
unframed, torn, trying
to roll himself into something
to be swung at heads.
                                Hello, it's your glazed self,
calling collect: 'Quit moping, losing & go get in
the graph, get in the graph! Suit up ... wear specs,
even!' It's said Melbourne's more subterranean
than Sydney, and so the coach carps on:
'Learn the ropes; learn to shimmy,
to swim the crawlspace …' But all you've
picked up are these road-closure stylings,
these rainy days.
                        How the body lingers
through days & won't listen to sleep,
almost like a 5 y.o., his parents parked in front
of late TV, & how, from a secluded step
on the stairs, he bears witness as
familyroom walls, overridden,
operate as light-traps.

                                    [Remember the first
time you stayed up to watch *Star Wars*?
'Daddy, what's a tractor beam?' Otherwise
everything made perfect sense: Force,
darkside, straws of power
flapped at the night. 'Luke,
you've switched off your targeting computer!'
Finding the vein, slimeball cowboy whooping
it home, the hottest car in the galaxy &
his wookie tough who couldn't handle
the heady stench of youth –
that overkeen stench.
                                    Still makes sense
30 years & 3 bottles later. Vader was always

your favourite figurine, the red retractable
light-sabre in his arm, like an overwound
lipstick. You liked to remove the weapon,
leave a tunnel leading through his hand –
the kind of lightless passage
where a father's kindness might nest.]

A bottle smashed upon kitchen tiles, its
neck still intact, is a kindred spirit: a poet!
You know that something goes here,
something *goes*. And maybe all the worlds
are real, just that this one got badly stung
by beauty (a wasp trying to tough its way
out of your t-shirt).
                    Even this pissed, you can dial
the dealer, spit 'I'm keen, can I get involved?'
at the receiver. Affirmative. You pass out safe
in the knowledge.

III - ***Alchemy***

You've succumbed. Tall Poppy,
they crave to say you've over-stepped.
Don't go too far. Stay too far. Settle
your petals against the sand; today's
a hot one on ego beach. Where we
can see, between the flags!
Swim on a rope.
                    How'd you expect us
to eat all this? What,
weren't you thinking?
What *weren't* you thinking?
                         Too long
in the kitchen, sniffling;
we want to feel your pain
but not forever. Brett,
it seemed someone was missing,
was not listening.
                      Your rockstar
mirrorgazes; hallucinating
momentary masterpieces,
blown away as studio dust
or shot up as lunch.
                         You
painted our waiting,
expectations in exquisite detail.

We've been tailgating you,
true, your faulty tail lights.

A work of ambition,
Icarus flightpath: alchemy
as perfective art of knowing,
as the impossible. Ambition's
there waving, hollering,
drowning in world. *It* writ large.

porn

i.e. where sex is a form of greeting begins with the basics tits
blowjobs etc stalking the elusive chase-thrill until chore of
the addict quest to out-gross you underperform no wonder
you
wonder why not bring the drugs in front of the camera the
post-shoot bloods cramps visits to quacks gynos & cashola
cut on desks in shoebox low-rent offices strewn with adult
store novelties stockpiled microwave dinners actress
ephemera industry awards
matter of fact that's been milked
seek & ye shall seek what you want's a free pass cultivating
mind dirtier than mysterious mid-rock-festival portaloo
discovered by timetravellers allegedly researching lives of
beggars & toms in 17th century london squalor
oops this was
unplanned uh whatever your day off home alone an
exercise in deletion the browser undone a cloaking
device clear history clear private data seeding the
afterfade you mindless gutless pointless

apology

sorry for the slow reply

i've been sick again,
spitting air,
crawling town without a face

(*a face no longer valid*)

hungry words flock
to define me:
'cut-price', 'reheated', 'uneven' …

so uneven i've been cutting
around the gardens rather than through
(fear fresh breath of pines
will make me retch)

scoped by a list of eyes,
tailed by some voodoo priest
giving off his dark light

no call for music, food

mostly hide tight
up in this one-window bedsit
flicking switches
experimenting with the light

gazing down
at the playhard kids
rewiring themselves,
scalping offworld passes

they're prepped
to ambush me with scissors,
milk the meds out

hope they'll accept this
small peace offering:
a freshly picked posey
of eyelashes

Still Life

Siddhārtha Gautama, the Buddha,
sits atop the left speaker
above the TV, VCR, DVD player,
CDs, home vids,
the music & films made meek by our rejection,
the Playstation, games cartridges,
busted console controllers.

The Buddha waits atop the left speaker;
atop the right speaker is a Dalek figurine
armed with pushbutton
for 5 different sound effects
& a manipulable eye.

Berlin

The West controlled the U-Bahn. Underground train lines passed under the wall at certain points. Passenger trains from the West would pass through 'ghost stations' in the East, never stopping at these.

*

The communications tower spiking out of Alexanderplatz still casts the old omniscient spell at night, red eyelets flashing over the grey grid below. Socialist system a torn web still dangling from housing blocks, the eastern Rathaus. In the former GDR, kids were herded into group potty sessions to sow the seeds of collectivism.

*

Chunks of city scattered amongst derelict blocks … may never be de-fragged. Temples falling into disuse. Underground clubs in abandoned vaults and warehouses; pulsar strobes ghosting on sweat, shaved heads, concrete.

*

One dark dividing wall to split the brain of a city. Graffiti coats the surviving segments.

*

The opening of the wall was a bureaucratic slip – a rogue document inserted to sabotage the machinery. Paper jam. At the press conference, without pausing to consider the words or their meaning, the official read out the memo.

chapel st

lemon, water, sun, saliva

day spins into hubcap

drowsed / stun-gun sun

so coloured up, the crave district

'... you fkn loser ...'

overdress & fuzz w/ desire

rear denim of 2 thin boys-in-love

street smokes, spits

what a postcard

someone's *nonna* sucks from KFC cup

fume of Marlboro

Natasha is a party

rushed heels

cross against lights phone clammed to ear

our waiter = pretentious wanker

the pointing tongue

coffee versus boredom

dresscoding

lining up outside Sugar Lounge under
conspicuous surveillance parasols rope
barriers please stow all attitudes at home
as if getting past brick of a bouncer wasn't
enough gender selection no hoodies immediate
access for the 'club babe' persona you
refuse to cultivate remaining true to
your otherness /
                        a studied ugliness no
sportswear of any description no
entry for all-male groups down the
rabbithole a privilege no guarantees
non-members turned away (with the
exception of cool clubwear) we're on
the guest list can you pick the plus-
one self-proclaimed doorbitch smiles us
in (average spend on alcohol £32.70)
(more for males) first we'd better
define conspicuous consumption
designer shoes ok /
                            lucky we know Jim
the promoter & Zane the DJ's a 16yo
prodigy 'course he's not allowed to buy
himself a drink /
                        these clubs such comic strips
thought balloons packed in tight many
frames to a page club drugs & drug clubs
Britain's night-time economy (NTE) the
flawless cocktail at £35,000 a pop consists of
a large measure of Louis XII Cognac half a
bottle of Cristal champagne brown sugar
angostura bitters flakes of edible 24-carat gold leaf
& at the bottom of the crystal glass
an 11-carat white diamond ring

notes on status

ha survive in a corporate office
without actually working (just
live there, haunt the espresso
machine)

see brother, *la revolution* begins on every page, in
every line

in gel caps /
the deepest blues

only to find that
nothing beards us like a lack
of ritual responsibilities

a life of not being able to
pop a balloon with a stick of celery

(not the place itself but your slim scared imaginings of)

like spring racing carnival,
fashions in the field yet
another vocabulary for
status to shake around in ...

deep in the bowels of
some corporate tent or other
you realise luxury is irresistible,
has its own set of 'classique' emotions

& one day,
with a dab of brio and your lucky haircut,
you could have your very own war

(thief!)

sharps (warding remix / after Nathan Moore)

There's a booklet called *Patient Rights*, which no one has read. Ceiling-mounted cameras raise conversation from its natural pitch by a semitone. Count the kinds of innocuous: white walls, a small set of lies played back to placate. For some of us the timetable remains mysterious, opaque; it approaches the divine. Fluorescent tube flashes code; spasmodic pain. Clipboards held towards white coats, shieldlike. Conspiring to dull us; that's my theory. Ticking off the codeine. The sharps (syringe, paper clips, knife) stored in micro-lockers. Some inmates bemoan the lack of music. Keys carried by orderlies provide semi-regular percussion. Padded footfalls. The door's alarmed; red pulsing bulb. When a car pulls up outside we set our foreheads on the glass. We ogle with the sincerity of children. The muscled orderlies arriving to move us on, their strides replicated on the monitors. Such incidents are all we have. Sometimes manhandled, somctimes a needle pierces.

down slow (song of samsara)

naked
beneath the drugs
this is what I am

this is my face:

skin torn up
like carpet,
pair of choking eyes

have to get sick
        to slow down

standing in the quickfire
lanes of dust
grabbing at particles

my hands
trying to eat clouds

the roads between us
the fish of light
the millions

have to get sick to slow down,
freeze the eyelake over

see the fish of light
frozen swimmers
a library of ice

let's learn to swim down here
while we're dark

bodies solved

our bodies much older
than we, than we think

have to get sick
to glimpse you
you
not some death girl
forearms awarded
parallel wounds

(you were laying new roads
with the knife)

skin torn up
like carpet,
pair of choking eyes

this is what you are (too)

beneath the drugs
down slow

A train, outbound

It takes minutes to leave the city. But to leave the city, mentally …

There are always nervous questions prior to departure. You must peel these off.

'See this industrial district? It has fled nature.'

Likewise seeing writing as avoidance; a rehearsal; opting for conversation with yourself. Living at a great distance.

The houses have satellite dishes as standard; ears to the wind. Powerline towers, like posts of an enormous fence. These are and are not 'life-conductors'.

Fields in which to expand, cease? As if cities were centres of forgetting. Gazing out the window, I swim the wild grass.

hands / office

this is Modern Art: / motivational / poster of the pyramids captioned 'Achievement' / the sky absent, savagely cropped / (how to measure achievement when the sky is absent?)

*

across the open plan / cool paint-tones emit calm / it's 'too nice a day' / sun nothing but hindrance / wimp blinds / glare-stained monitors / staff listless / doing time behind / heat-panes / call logged re: the aircon / drip workflow / has sprung a lake

*

Bruce, who *loves* Friday drinks / is not alone / after-work trains become sparsely passengered / & this is / isn't this / who you are today / a drowner / 'Gabe 'n' me are hitting the Deep End after work …' / your brains / your talent / you could be / '… anyone else?'

*

cubicles, 'pods' / officespace sugared with commercial FM / looped playlist / *American Idol*? No, I don't / I am an island / correction: shoal / mousy Support Analyst / acned / phonecall evader / in shooting out the apartment / this morning, toast in hand / neglected to carry enough / defeat music / to see out the day

*

Bruce is seasoned / old hand, old hands / wandering / knows where to sit, stand / for best access / the bar, ripe officegirls / sloshed against a washroom wall / No sorry I'm feeling / a little married / tonight

*

dead links on the intranet / What's the name, the girl from Accounts / the off-tap? / I'll copy you in / something wicked this way / brushed by tiesilk / Are you hitting on / we'll put it to the bored / bang on about / the ethics, if you like / 'These aren't the right minutes!' / I smell a / Steering Committee / duty-free cologne / & bulk-price handwash

*

two weeks pass / Bruce gets taken out / to lunch at the brasserie / I forget, what's the name of that swank-shack on Bourke? / clears his desk upon return / then escorted by security / heaving boxes labeled 'Fragile' / out the revolving doors / a chance slap of wind / scattering flock / of white papers / to blot the gutter rain

charisma

When was the last time you faked charisma?

Were you wasted?

Profiling your interests for a dating site?
('wild parties, latin dancing, balloon sculpture')

Sometimes making a fake is a waste, like breaking a lake or trying to pick up in a pickup.

*

The way we are a couple of days after getting loved up on pills is the opposite of charisma:
our faces deserted, all but the most animal entertainment fails;
all is lost
(until rediscovered).

'Suicide Tuesday': your manager wears charisma like headdress feathers of a Sioux chief seen reflected on your monitor while he peers, arms folded, behind you.

(If you were reborn as an officeworker you'd hope to be blind; who needs the acquiescent eyes, carcinogens, lab-tested décor?)

Figure only some freak emergency can save you; daydream that in some corner of hyperspace (hmm ... looks like a gym ...?) disaster has dropped:
trampling hordes / malfunctioning alarms / charisma leaking everywhere

k. rudd

as if he might correct himself
by repeating himself, coming over
all churchy & austere (such hubris
no longer confined to election years) to snub
kerry o'brien's smile, knowing our access
to such duplicities is inconsistent, fleeting,
forever wrongfooted, a series of tangential
curves towards & away from a single
point, as per television's 'routings', as astride
a parent's knee a boy begins to lie

stock

tabs on what others are
doing perhaps leaving
you sipping the wake of
their excellence time
to rethink the tint of
your calling card &
all manoeuvres as
pedestrian evasive
action stalling tactics
you were always a
next time boy your
room off-limits to
the living its abject
stuffincss sock stenches
those unwanted wanted
things your hibernation
hoard & feigning
upheavals to buy more
time to yourself the
retreat into trivia to
dull & dilute this
friendlessness perfected

Inferno

& when you finally touch down
in hell
(no red carpet)
the coffee'd better be strong.
Hungover-horny & (shit!) your sunglasses
left at home in a jacket pocket.
Of all the things to be without ...
Sterling Morrison, Ray Charles & Joey Ramone,
all smarter than you (on this score),
look godlike standing round in shades
(still!)
The future's so bright, etc.
It's funny, Lucifer's looking a lot
like Danny Tenaglia these days.
Guess he's always hoarded the killer tunes.
Had them all
back at the tree, in snaketime. Brokered ever since.
So here's the rub:
there's drugs everywhere
but no painkillers
or sleepers.
Figure pretty quick that you won't
be sleeping 'til … who knows …
Judgement?
But by then your bender will've
gathered such momentum that
you'll've forgotten everything
important – even what they say
about the wicked. Anyway, it's true. Plus
they're out of ice.

Night of the Living Dead
(after the 1968 George A Romero film)

Boarding up all windows and doors, using whatever we can find. Breaking up furniture. Lock ourselves inside the house. An excuse to break taboos. The sick little girl turns into a zombie, consumes her dead father's flesh, then stabs her mother repeatedly with a cement trowel, killing her. The moral to the story: don't make fun of the dead, especially in a cemetery. They have us outnumbered. Tom & Judy burn to death when a gasoline spillage causes their car to catch fire. Zombies feast on their barbecued flesh. Recall a fast food advertisement, the glowing family trying to out-excite each other across the table. If you're waiting for the real enemy to show up, damn it, you'll be waiting all night. If we lock ourselves in the cellar there'll be no way out. What, you think it's sexual? The deep, glossy black of blood in black & white films. Reflective liquid. Won't find a better man than a black man. Trust you to mistake him for a zombie … Disaster in the middle of nowhere; a haunting lack of sirens. There's always a token naked zombie whenever we see them marauding as a group. Not even thinly veiled. The radio & TV emergency announcements are so, so camp: 'Thousands of office and factory workers are being urged to stay at their places of employment, not to make any attempt to get to their homes.' Shoot on sight. A situation where 'anything' can be justified, or where justification is moot. We see a slap across the face on screen; it matters that it's simulated? She's hysterical & therefore of no use to us. You have to laugh: it's a horror flick. The zombies massing to devour the woman, leaning in, stretching their hands through holes in the wall. We know a ghoulish hand when we see one – but how? The zombies are hideously slow, but strong enough to overturn a car. Temporary fix: flaming torch fends them off. Walking political allegories. The men argue over the best options for staying alive until help arrives. You call these survival instincts? An abject failure of the system.

Seven Sevens

#1

‘There is no enemy.’ Oh?
Recall how I howled, kicking
the wind. Untranquilised.
In at least two minds.
Magpie leaves a scratch (paranoia
being merely a heightened state
of awareness) on the forehead.

#3

We can always get more.
For reassurance.
Looking for something selfish,
read the field.
‘People prefer things over people.’
‘Glad I’m not dualistic
like you guys.’

#4

The word again
is ‘interface’.
Conversant with.
Our heads lie before us.
(‘Drown inside’.)
I go hooded.
Meds.

#13

naive, curious,
had all ports open;
trojan’s bloodless coup.
tomorrow sees you
pixel-mining
extremer, extremer.
(words wilt/fail).

#14

They mistake words for things.
Won't say 'I' any more –
how could you?
An artist wants a world different,
different again from how she finds it.
Those profiting from their careful errors.
An exhibition of picture frames.

#17

Couldn't return her
gaze with a straight
phrase. Got hoaxed. Casualties
of noise. Performed upon. Your
chauffeured defiance / closet
hetero- &
other violations.

#18

microclimates within the mall

muzak / 'toons / migraine

enter the store, expect service
to envelop you

pushy, nasal intimidation / dis-
proportionate response

such indoor behaviour

faulty

your speed-reading eyes
stalled by things I don't have names for:
birds, trees ... 'nature stuff'

so we invent names from our lexicon:
banking bird, valium tree

our poems detail
glitches of perception,
are loose & easy,
repel ghosts

For Edwin

We have always been as weightless as this.

Our modest collection of questions.

Holes full of nets; nets full of holes.

No waiting: all things are present.

Eye observes itself.

self-portrait (with wires, city, no clothes)

i am open
and open
and open

(the city, sleepless)

city, be slow with me,
city ... slow down ...
(i love you)

though back home on my body
hair grows like wild grass

back home in my eye
something quick and approximate
(a snapshot
of the whole perfect whole?)

you asked to see a photo, but
i asked for paper
to write on

am i colour-code wires, ant colony,
wide area network,
landmass seen from airplane window (?)

am i sub-atomic ghost (?)

i am those
and those
and those

(sometimes i
look very familiar)

am i the words
which with use
became unusable (?)

the gap between
inbreath, outbreath (?)

i want to plant lamps

i'm walking around
no armour, no cloak

(i look pretty strange)

i am yes
and yes
and yes

and here
and here

(i'm so glad
you could make it)

Notes on the poems

Vipassanā (p. 20): The literal translation of vipassanā (Pali) is 'insight'. Vipassanā also refers to a form of meditation practice, i.e. insight meditation.

draft wording for revolution : from balcony at Blue Train Café (p. 21): 'hybrid seeds': 'Hybrid seed cannot be saved, as the seed from the first generation of hybrid plants does not reliably produce true copies, therefore, new seed must be purchased for each planting.'
(Source: http://en.wikipedia.org/wiki/Hybrid_seed)

'juicer linebackers': linebackers are members of the defense in American football. A 'juicer' is someone who uses steroids to 'bulk up'.

power ballad (p. 22): This poem references the song 'Pure Morning' by Placebo, from the album *Without You I'm Nothing* (Virgin Records).

post-rock (p. 23): 'Post-rock is a genre of rock music characterized by the use of musical instruments commonly associated with rock music, but using rhythms, harmonies, melodies, timbre, and chord progressions that are not usually found in rock tradition. It is the use of 'rock instrumentation' for non-rock purposes. Practitioners of the genre's style typically produce instrumental music.' (Source: http://en.wikipedia.org/wiki/Post-rock) Bands labelled 'post-rock' include Godspeed You! Black Emperor, Mogwai, Sigur Rós, Explosions in the Sky, and Tortoise.

departing (p. 30): 'the Swan', i.e. the Swan River.

retreat (pp. 34-38): This poem is based on a ten-day Vipassanā meditation retreat which I undertook in December/January 2007-08, observing a 'vow of silence' throughout.

Portrait of Ledong Qui (p. 46): 'baijiu' = a variety of Chinese white liquor, usually between 40-60% proof, in this case distilled from sorghum.

scratches (pp. 51-54): '*E. Coli*' = *Escherichia coli***,** a bacterium commonly found in the lower intestine of warm-blooded organisms. Some strains can cause serious food poisoning in humans, and have been responsible for product recalls. Species such as cows and pigs may harbour toxigenic bacteria, shedding them in their faeces, from which they may be spread to humans. Flesh can become contaminated during slaughter and butchering, and organisms can be thoroughly mixed into beef when it is ground into hamburger. These issues are discussed in the documentary *Food, Inc*. (Magnolia Pictures). I have adapted this information from the following *Wikipedia* pages: http://en.wikipedia.org/wiki/E._coli and http://en.wikipedia.org/wiki/Escherichia_coli_O157:H7.

mnml (p. 55): 'mnml' / 'minimal' = minimalist techno, i.e. a form of electronic dance music.

Three Brett Whiteleys (pp. 56-59): reproductions of the three Brett Whiteley paintings which inspired these poems can be viewed here: http://www.brettwhiteley.org/alchemy_and_more

Berlin (p. 63): 'U-Bahn' = underground rapid transit rail system.

'Rathaus' = town hall (literally 'council house').

'GDR' = German Democratic Republic, i.e. the former socialist state also known as East Germany.

chapel st (p. 64): '*nonna*' = Italian for 'grandmother'

dresscoding (p. 65): This poem owes a considerable debt to Phil Hadfield's article 'From Threat to Promise: Nightclub 'Security', Governance and Consumer Elites' in the *British Journal of Criminology*, and his presentation at the Club Health conference, Ibiza 2008.

sharps (p. 67): this is a remix of Nathan Moore's poem 'Sharps'. The remix was produced as part of our collaborative 'remix exchange'. Nathan's poem can be read here: http://disorder1313.wordpress.com/2009/02/03/sharps-revised/

Inferno (p. 76): Sterling Morrison played guitar in The Velvet Underground. Danny Tenaglia is a New York-based DJ known for his marathon stints behind the decks (20-hour sets are not unusual for him).

Publication Credits (Australia unless noted)

'drowse': published in *bambikino* #9, November 2008.

'drive-thru': published in *Mascara* #1, April 2007.

'cashed': published in *hutt* #2.5, May 2007.

'the breaking': published in *Page Seventeen* #3, April 2006.

'post-rock': published in *Otoliths* #9, May 08; broadcasted on *Wordsalad* (US), September 2009.

'the masculine': published in *Otoliths* #14, August 2009.

'development': published in *foam:e* #7, March 2010.

'the days write themselves': published in *The Age*, March 2010.

'repackaging evil': published in *Snorkel* #9, April 2009.

'forkhead': published in *Sein und Werden* (UK), April 2009.

'café date': published in *Overland*, Overload Poetry Festival online feature, September 2009, and in *Miscellaneous Voices: Australian Blog Writing*, April 2010.

'Portrait of Ledong Qui': published in *Mascara* #1, April 2007.

'free of the fear of freedom': exhibited at Federation Square, Melbourne for the Overload Poetry Festival, September 2009.

'porn': published in *Otoliths* #14, August 2009.

'apology': published in *mad swirl* (US), December 2009.

'Berlin': published in *Shadowtrain* (UK) October 2009; broadcasted on *Wordsalad* (US) May 2009.

'chapel st': published in *bambikino* #9, November 2008.

'notes on status': published in *foam:e* #7, March 2010.

'down slow': published in *Poetry Sz* (NZ) #25, March 2008.

‘A train, outbound’: published in *Shadowtrain* (UK), October 2009.

‘hands / office’: published in *[untitled]* #1, September 2009.

‘charisma’: published in *bambikino* #9, November 2008.

‘k. rudd’: this poem was written as part of a collaborative project. Derek Motion solicited ten-line poems from twenty poets, then rearranged the resulting 200 lines into the collage-poem ‘Before Elapsing’, as published in *Overland* #200, August 2010.

‘stock’: published in *Thirteen Myna Birds* (US), September 2009.

‘Inferno’: published in *mad swirl* (US), October 2009.

‘Night of the Living Dead’: published in *Otoliths* #14, August 2009.

‘Seven Sevens’: #3, #4, #14 and #17 published in *Otoliths* #16, February 2010. #1 and #18 published in *Some Sonnets*, August 2010.

‘faulty’: published in *Otoliths* #12, February 2009; broadcasted on *Wordsalad* (US), May 2009.

‘For Edwin’: published in *The Cartier Street Review* (Canada), February 2009.

‘self-portrait (with wires, city, no clothes)’: published in *Verandah* #22, September 2007.

* Some of the poems were also originally published on my blog (www.stuhatton.net) and in the ‘Words’ forum on Bluelight (http://www.bluelight.ru/vb/forumdisplay.php?f=62).

www.ingramcontent.com/pod-product-compliance
Ingram Content Group UK Ltd.
Pitfield, Milton Keynes, MK11 3LW, UK
UKHW051129260726
13967UKWH00010B/2935

9 781446 63133